There Once Was
A Cat From Nantucket...

BLUE BOX BOOKS

There Once Was A Cat From Nantucket
All Rights Reserved
© 2015 K.A. Thompson

No part of this book may be reproduced or transmitted in any form or by any means without permission in writing from the publisher.

Published by Blue Box Books

www.blueboxbooks.com
ISBN 978-1-932461-35-0

Printed in the United States of America

There Once Was
A Cat From Nantucket...

Poetry by

MAX THOMPSON

Also by Max Thompson

The Psychokitty Speaks Out: Diary of a Mad Housecat

The Psychokitty Speaks Out: Something of Yours Will Meet a Toothy Death

The Rules: A Guide For People Owned By Cats

Bite Me (A Memoir of Sorts)

Epistle: A Love Letter

Visit Max online at his blog The Psychokitty Speaks Out
http://psychokitty.blogspot.com

Books one of his people (K.A. Thompson) wrote:

Charybdis
As Simple As That
Finding Father Rabbit
The King and Queen of Perfect Normal
The Flipside of Here
It's Not About the Cookies
Rock the Pink

Visit K.A. Thompson online at her blog
http://kathompson.blogspot.com

This book is for you
And for her and for him
It's for Stormy and Princess
And that one dog named Jim

It's for kitties whose names
I never will know
And for dogs and for people
And earthworms that glow

It's my deepest thinks
And for me not a rarity
The monies I make
Will go to a charity.

> Yes, I am a cat
> An intelligent feline
> Writing just for you

"Max," you say, "you're just a cat
"How can you write at all?

"How do you think, how do you tell
"The stories from your mind?"

It's simple, you know.
I have a human; I dictate.

Duh.

Once upon a time
When I was all but two
I wrote a spiffy, nifty book
And I wrote it just for you

And then again
When I was three
I wrote another 'cuz
People asked, you see

As time went on
More books I did write
Often did I toil away
Late, late, into the night

I told you the Rules
I gave you advice
And now I have poetry
Isn't that nice…?

Of course it is
I'm sharing my thinks
In lovely form
And none of it stinks.

I hope.
I mean, I think it's all right.
Just *like* me, dammit.

"Dear Max, I love you,"
I hear that all the time.
"Please be my everything.
"Please please please be mine."

But doods, you know I love you all
And all of you the same
I cannot tie myself down
To just one friend; that's lame.

Well, not *lame*, for sure, that just sounds mean
But it's something I can't do.
Let's just admit I'm not that kind
And pretend I'm here for you.

Well, not like THAT
That wouldn't be fair
To her and her and him
Oh Bast, please tell me

Why the heck I'm so awesome that everyone wants to be with me and if they can't be *with* me they want to *be* me. It's an awful lot of pressure.

What's for dinner?
Is it real live fresh dead cow?
Is it real live fresh dead chicken?
Is it real live fresh dead shrimp?

Tell me what's for dinner.
No, show me!
Show me what's for dinner!
Aw. You're having pasta.

Disappointment.
That's what's for dinner.

No, I did not take your food.
You got up and went to the fridge,
And left on the table a piece of bacon.
The rules are the rules and the rule is:
If a person gets up from the table,
And leaves a piece of bacon,
It is no longer his bacon,
But belongs to the kitty.

My bowl.
There's a space at the bottom of my bowl.
There's a space where no food touches.
My bowl.
My bowl has no food.
No, the pieces at the edge don't count.
Those are the orphans of the crunchy food world.
Orphans don't get eaten.
They get saved.
My bowl.
My bowl.
My bowl.
Is empty.

Creeping, crawling, it looked me in the eye
This mess I see, you called it Chicken Pie
And I also have this really weird hunch
That you somehow think that it's just *your* lunch.

I love that kind of food
It's wet and it stinks
And it tastes so good
I think I could eat it every day
Maybe twice on Sundays
You noticed I love that food,
And bought me twenty seven cans
So now I can't eat it
Not at all.
Not ever again.
You ruined it for me.

The slow cooker thingy is not a crock.
It is the giver of real live fresh dead things
Cooked to juicy, wondrous perfection.
It's a pot that holds close all the things I love
Heated up all day, making the house smell
Of amazing meaty goodness.
Whoever named it should be shot
Or at least given a wedgie of the atomic kind.
Because the slow cooker thingy is not a crock.

I was asleep
But I smelled bacon
And then I heard the sound of bacon
Sizzling and popping
The way bacon
Is wont to do.
So I got myself up
And wandered down the hall
And went into the kitchen
Because that's where bacon
Lives and Dies
And drains the grease
On a paper towel on a plate
While waiting on the counter.
But in the kitchen
There was no bacon
Not that I could see
And the Woman was just sitting
In the living room
Watching the TV
Pretending that the aroma

Was not hanging in the air.
So I sat and I waited
Because I know that somewhere
There is a plate of bacon
And sometime soon
She will get up
And try to eat some of the bacon
And I will be waiting
Patiently
I know that she's hiding it
Probably in the microwave
Knowing I can't open it
But once she takes it out
All bets are off
And I might feel the impulse
To run between her feet
And if she just happens
To drop a piece or two
I will be considerate
And clean up the mess for her.
Because I am a gentleman
And because, bacon.

When you are absent from the house
Thinking that I am here alone and lonely
Wondering where you are
And if you are coming home
Imagining me sitting by the window
Staring at the outside forlornly
Counting the ticks of the clock
The minutes feeling like so many hours
Until you come home again
Remember that I am not a dog
I am asleep in the closet
And I do not care if you are gone
As long as you're home
At Food O'Clock.

Once upon a time,
As midnight rolled around
I made my way down the hall,
Carefully, no sound.
I stalked my prey with extra care,
To fulfill an urgent wish
My stomach growled, propelling me:
Someone must fill my dish.

The sounds of sleep surrounded me
As I headed for the bed
And up I jumped, right on the spot,
The one beside her head.
I crouched in place, so very close
And said these words right in her ear:

MY DISH IS EMPTY
AND I NEED YOUR THUMBS
SO GET UP NOW AND FILL IT
YOU LAZY SLEEPING BUM.

And over she rolled and loudly she groaned
"It's three o'clock, furball,"
And once more she did moan,
Ignoring my starving self, making me wait
Turning that sliver of affection for her
Into something resembling hate.

But wait patiently I did; I let her go to sleep.
Just fifteen minutes later,
Closer to her did I creep.
WAKE UP WAKE UP WAKE UP WAKE UP
I NEED TO NOM RIGHT NOW!
But sleep she just kept doing, snoring human cow.

Waiting doesn't suit me, patience not my name
Starving isn't funny, hunger not a game.
So I did what just came naturally
To get her out of bed
I shoved my cold wet dripping nose
Into a hole inside her head.

And it totally worked, doods
It took like 5 hours but she got up and fed me.
I win.

You're not very nice, she said to me
In an email that was just that
You grumble and grouse and say things mean
And face it, you're kinda, well, fat.
On she complained, page after page
Saying things that were really unkind
So my feelings were hurt, pretty bad I must say
And revenge….it did enter my mind.
But often things aren't what they look like they are
And intentions not quite what they seem
And cruel words spoken in lengthy email
Are often just part of a dream.
To the Woman I said, sometimes when I sleep
I think things that just are not true
Of people and kitties and woofies galore
And once in a while even you.
But I don't understand how that mean email
Became such a part of my thinks
It never existed, not remotely for reals
That it's in my head frankly just stinks.
That happens, she said, when our brains aren't awake
And we're working through things not so clear

You're worried that people don't like you

So you're dreaming your way through that fear.

We all have dreams that surprise us

Filled with monsters and spiders and bugs

Mine is of Captain Kirk dressed like a lawyer

Chasing me, chasing me, looking for hugs.

For reals, she admitted, he haunts her at night

And this happens a few times a year

I never have figured it out, she did say

But like you, it's addressing a fear.

So I pondered that think and realized she was right

Dreams are night thinks and sort of a test

The worst one of mine is a years-long night terror

And looks much like a furry black Pest.

I do dream of my friends and of happy fun times

And of endless bowls of good food

So the not-often nightmares and self-doubting thinks

Are fine, 'cuz my life? It's amazingly good.

It did make me wonder about her,

The Woman and dream Denny Crane

It's proof to my long held opinion

There's something wrong with her brain.

So many times have you packed up your things

And strange people entered the house to take them away.

So many times did I suffer the journey
Days on end of "Are we there yet?" to be told "No."

So many times did I have to explore somewhere new
And get used to how it smelled and how it looked.

So many times did I go along without complaint
Because none of us had a choice and we had to go.

So now that there's a new chair and I have discovered it
I am not going to get up because you owe me this.

Go sit somewhere else.

I am not moving.
Ok, so after breakfast I went to take a nap
Because that is the natural order of things.
Eat, sleep, get up, poop, and then do it again.
But today after I took my nap
I got up and went to the living room
And everything was wrong.
The TV was in the not-TV room
And the chairs were in the not-TV room
But they belong in the TV room.

And the not-TV things that belong in the not-TV room
Were in the TV-room
And they were not facing the space
Where the TV should have been.

Now, the other cat thinks that while we were sleeping

The people up and moved,
That dreaded M-word,
Even after promising we would never move again
And that this is the house I will die in.
He didn't stop to consider
That our food dishes are where they belong
And the litter box is just where it should be
And only the TV and not-TV things have changed.
But I can hardly blame him for thinking that
Because no matter what
Moving my stuff around without warning
Is a not-nice thing to do.
Things were fine where they were
But I will not complain.
Because the truth is that rearranging the furniture
Is a whole lot better
Than moving me.

Nip.
Nip. Nip.
Nip. Nip. Nip.
Nip. Nip. Nip. Nip.
Nip. Nip. Nip. Nip. Nip.
Nip. Nip. Nip. Nip. Nip. Nip.
Nip. Nip. Nip. Nip. Nip. Nip. Nip.
Nip. Nip. Nip. Nip. Nip. Nip. Nip. Nip.
Nip. Nip. Nip. Nip. Nip. Nip. Nip.
Nip. Nip. Nip. Nip. Nip. Nip.
Nip. Nip. Nip. Nip. Nip.
Nip. Nip. Nip. Nip.
Nip. Nip. Nip.
Nip. Nip.
Nip.

The colors have sound
And the blue just turned red
The music that echoes
Is all in my head
This nip is amazing
It makes me feel fine
And the dragon in the kitchen
Helped eat the Silver Vine.

There are 37 toys in the toy basket
And 13 on the floor around it
And 19 in the other room
But I don't see my nip banana
I have nothing to play with.

My toy
My toy is over there
I am over here
I want that toy
It looks like a banana
Which I normally don't like
But it's filled with catnip goodness
And colors I can hear
It has music I can taste
And whispers that echo
But it is over there
And I am over here
And the floor is lava
And my paws are bare
Be a good person,
Fetch me my toy
You have shoes on
So your feet won't melt
I need that toy
I love that toy
That toy over there.

Yes, that was on the counter.
Now it is not.
Yes, I did it.
It is not my fault.
Yes, you really liked that thing.
But it is no more.
Yes, you're cleaning it up.
I don't have thumbs.
Yes, I will do it again.
Unless you put your krap away.

There's a mouse in my water dish.
I see it, there's no point in asking me about it.
Mice get thirsty and the dish is right there,
So what did you expect?
Sure, fish him out, I don't care.
He's probably had his fill.
But now he's all squishy and won't dry out right.
He'll smell in a day or two.
His nip innards will be moldy.
Go ahead, throw him out.
But I'll need a new one,
And he'll get thirsty, too.

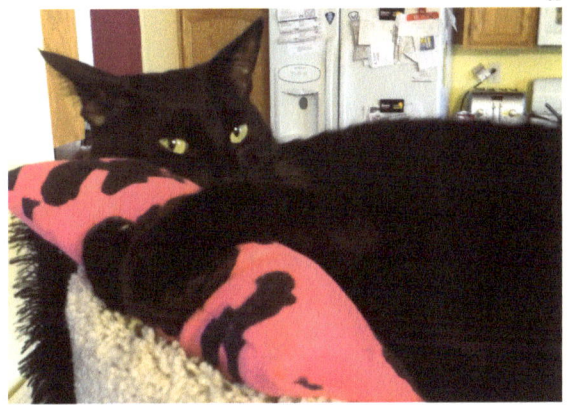

The other cat, he takes the toys
And covers them with spit.
The other cat, he drives me nuts
And makes me say Oh…

You understand, I know you do
You feel my unsaid plight.
I cannot type that word, you see
I'm told it's not polite.

But I would like a toy that's all my own
Just for a bit, unused
My life's one wish: a spiffy toy
That's never been abused.

Inside my house there lives another cat
No one asked me before they brought him home,
Before he began eating all my food
And usurping all my toys.

He chases me down the hallway
And wants to ride me like a pony
He has claws and uses them
And he bites me on the neck.

I was happy being an only cat
I don't know what they were thinking
I suppose they thought I was lonely
And would like the company.

The truth is that my deepest wish
A wish I whisper every year
On my birthday, even though I don't get cake
And there are no candles to blow out

I wish that he would calm the frakk down
And learn that OW means STOP
And NO means NO
And that I do not have a saddle on my back.

I never wish that he was gone
Because that would be, like, 10 kinds of wrong
He needs a place to live
And food to eat

I just wish for him to change a bit
And learn to not be mean
Hoping against hope
Because he's really not that bright.

He's not going anywhere
I know that and it's all right
But I wish they had asked me first
So I could have at least hidden some toys.

I watched the other cat
Run across the room
Jump up on the bookcase
Leap to the back of the chair
And then I watched him
Slide down to the seat
Then he soared to the sofa
And then pounced on a toy
That he'd left on the floor
I watched him run and run and run
And it made me tired
So I'm taking a nap
I deserve it
He's exhausting.

The other cat is really not that smart.
He doesn't understand feet
Or that they sometimes live in shoes
And he doesn't realize that feet are attached
To the legs of the people.
When they get new shoes
His little head explodes
And he backs up like a snake
Is creeping up on him.
He doesn't understand hands
And that those hands are attached
To the arms of the people.
If he's sitting on a lap and sees a finger twitch
He gets all bitey
And then doesn't know why
The person gets upset.
I've thought about telling him
That all those pieces and parts
Combine to make a whole person
And that his toothy things cause pain,
But he gets in trouble for it a lot
And that amuses me.

There's another other cat who lives here
But he stays in the giant litter box room
And he looks just like me.
I really like the other other cat
Because he doesn't eat my food
And he doesn't bomb the litter box.
He just stays there on the counter
And sniffs me back when I sniff him.
He's also very, very handsome.

The other cat, he has a name
When I heard it first I wasn't sure
Because "Buddha" didn't really fit
Someone who's Evil-wrapped-in-fur.

I protested; this isn't right
His being that name is deplorable
He's not that smart; he's not that nice
In fact…he's downright horrible.

He bit me on the dangly bits
And scratched close to my eyes
Rename him! I demanded
He's nothing close to wise.

So they swapped around some letters
And then settled on the truthy best
He is not Buddha, that gentle man:
His for-reals name is Buddah Pest.

When I was the most scared at the beginning
The day I was taken from a crying girl
And put into a car and driven away
With the world speeding past outside the window
And a tall person I only barely knew
Talking to me like I was going on a big adventure
I thought that was the end.

I did not know what an adventure really was
Or that it meant more than sitting in the car
Wondering what was happening
And why the crying girl let him take me
So I barely listened to him when he told me things
About the forever home I was going to
But I did hear him mention the dog.

What I knew was this:
I lived in a place and then I did not
And cars go fast and the sky does, too,
When it's outside the car window
And I knew that I was afraid and wanted to cry
But curling up in a tight little ball
Seemed like a very bad idea.

I told him to take me home
Once or twice or three times
All he would say was that it would be okay;
The house was big and there was room to run
And then the car stopped and went quiet
He got out and opened my door
So did the front door to the house.

I was scared I was scared I was scared
This giant woman in floppy clothes
Bounding down the step
Walking quickly across the grass
And she was looking right at me
Not at the tall guy who had taken me from the crying girl
And she squealed "He's so beautiful!"

I was scared but not so scared but scared
Paying attention to all the things around me
There was food for me and only me
And the dog was on a leash
Two hundred times they said I was beautiful
Then showed me my new home
I was not as scared.

It took us all some time to get there
To that place where nothing is new
Where familiar is comfortable
And I thought that life was pretty sweet
Something to want to wake up for
So every morning I wake the woman up
With sweet songs of my people.

The days have grown longer
And yet have become shorter
And in between them we have moved a lot
Finding places to explore
I learned that being scared is not so bad
Even when new things are sometimes Big
But often, so often, being scared takes you home.

If I had thumbs, I could rule the world.
I could open doors and sniff the Great Outside.
I could open windows, and invite inside
All the sun puddles and breezes.

If I had thumbs, I could rule the world.
I could change the channel on the TV
I could watch whatever I wanted
Doctor Who and Animal Planet.

If I had thumbs, I could rule the world.
I could open cans all on my own
I could have great feasts
And invite all my friends.

If I had thumbs, I could rule the world.
I could do anything I wanted
I could do it now, and I think I will
Starting with a nap.

A winter's day
I'm full of food
And warm from the fire
The curtains are open
Gray skies I can see
It's beautiful
Life is good
I'm sleepy
And I don't want to move
But I have to poop
Dammit.

You hurt my feelings, but what did I do?
I sucked it up like the mancat I am.
I composed myself until the upset faded.
And then I barfed right into your shoe.

It has eight legs
And a billion beady eyes.

It creeps along the pillow
Much to your surprise.

You jump so high and girly-squeal:
That speed is quite the feat

For someone who has reached your size
And then you point and tell me, "Eat!"

As if I'd really nom the guts
Of gross yet juicy things

Or bite into its belly soft
And risk the part that stings.

So I just pull off its legs
Which makes you kind of mad

Just wait a minute, you'll get your want
It's almost dead; be glad

I do not, will not, eat the bugs
Or other squishy things

I'll amputate the tiny legs
And bite off little wings

So lay back down and try to sleep,
Or lay there with eyes wide

I do not care, I truly don't;
I won't commit insecticide

I did not barf on the floor
I barfed on your t-shirt instead.
I figured you could
Just toss it in the washer
So, you're welcome.

I also cleared off the counter
All those pieces of junk mail
And the paper towels and four pens
There was a bottle, too
So, you're welcome.

I noticed that you changed the sheets
And they were absent of any fur
I know you like to be warm
So I rolled all over and re-furred them
So, you're welcome.

And this morning, to be nice
I kicked half of the litter out of the box
So now there is less to scoop
I do all of this stuff for you
So, you're welcome.

Yes, I am on the floor, on my back.
No, I am not airing out my junk.
Yes, you may touch my chest.
No, you may not poke my belly.
Yes, I like the chin rubs
No, I do not like that long rub.
Yes, will bite if you linger
No, I don't care if that upsets you.

No, I do not want to go outside.
Outside is outside and outside is not good.
My food and toys and everything else
Are inside, and inside is inside and inside is good.
But if you leave the front door open
I might have to stick my head out
And sniff the outside, just to be sure.
And if I smell something nasty and alluring
I might have to check it out.
So close the damn door.
You're letting the outside get in.

Don't tell me I'm fluffy.
Don't tell me I'm Rubenesque.
Don't tell me I'm just a big boy.
Don't cover up who I am.
Don't pretend I'm something I'm not.

I am fat.
I am fat.
I am fat.
I am 18 pounds.
I am fat.

That's ok.
I am awesome.
I am glorious.
Feed me.
Feed me now.

Look.
The Internet told me
If I fits
I sits.
You have a box
I would have it.
I need to see
If I fits.
If I do
I will sits.
Or lays.
I could use a nap.

The stabby guy is the stabby guy
Because he stabs things
And I don't want to be near a guy
Who is going to stab me.
The stabby guy also has cold things
That he places where
Cold things should never be.
So if you take me to the stabby guy
Thinking I might be sick
Just remember my mighty skill
I can poop at will.
I will poop on the table
I will poop on the floor
I will poop on the stabby guy
And then I will do it again.
I will also poop in the car
And in the blue plastic tomb
That you take me there in.
And make no mistake
If I get the chance
I will also poop on you.

It is summer time
I can see it outside my window
And because we live where we live
That means the grass is almost dead
And the trees are unhappy
With droopy limbs
And curling leaves.
I love summer time
For the sun puddles on my floor
And the warms that eek through the windows
Plus the cold air blowing thingy

That lives in my ceiling.
But I am ready for winter time
When it sometimes rains
And the grass turns green
And the trees turn happy
When they stretch their limbs
And their leaves uncurl
Before falling to the ground.
I love winter time
For the warms that come out of the fireplace
And the long pants the Woman wears
Making her lap not so squishy.
There is still a lot of summer left
And the hots to go with it
I will always love it
But will welcome the cold,
Biting, nipply cold.
I have fur.
Sucks to be you if you don't.

My ears.
My ears are screaming.
My ears are bleeding.
My ears are offended.
My ears are twitching.
Please stop that noise.
Please stop right now.
Please stop before my head explodes.
Please stop.
You cannot sing.

There's a treadmill
And there's a bicycle
But the bicycle doesn't go anywhere
There's another thingy
With giant feet-pads on it
It all looks very spendy
And I'm not sure why
They need so many
Clothes racks.

My one true love is not something I seek
I love to love everyone the same
So I told that girl kitty I would take her out
On the second Tuesday of next week.

Every week she emails and asks me
How many more Tuesdays until the next?
And it started, like three years ago
It's the bigger picture she can't see.

I don't think that this makes her sad
She has her hope, she likes me still
But I just can't tie myself to just one kitty
I love you all…so please don't be mad.

Closets are a wonderful thing
Where the people can hang their second skins
Creating a curtain of invisible
Behind which I can peacefully nap
Because the other cat is not quite bright
And does not grasp that I might be there
Trying to get away from him
And sometimes the people leave their second skins
In a pile on the closet floor
Making a comfy, stinky bed for me
It smells like them and is almost as soft
As their squishy laps tend to be
But without the whole getting up to pee thing
Or the whole waking me up for chin skritches thing.
There are two closets that I really love
One is in the big bedroom

But the door to that is often closed
And one is at the end of the hallway
The door to that is usually closed, too,
But if I ask just right and eleventy times
The Woman will open it for me
And there's a towel on a low shelf just for me.
The other cat sometimes wants in there
But not very often, which is good
So I can nap in peace for hours
Then get up and get a snack and a drink
Only to go back to snooze some more.
But what I don't like about the closets,
The only real drawback to going in.
Is the stupid things the people say
When they see me coming out.

Let us discuss this:
Elevator Butt.
You take two fingers,
Tickle by my tail
And up my hind quarter goes.
You find this funny
My quivering skin,
Twitching tail,
Asterisk in the air.
I don't know
What to make of it
I hate it,
Yet I don't,
And I want to bite you,
Yet I won't.
It happens every time

Even when I think
Nope, I will not
Let my butt get
Higher than my head.
So when you're lying down
I knead your back
At pretty much
The same spot,
But the only thing
That ever happens
Is a fart,
And it's not even mine.
This is so unfair.
My butt
Has a mind of its own.

High places.
I love high places.
I used to jump to high places.
Now I look up
And remember when
And wonder if I still can
Then I sigh
And look for places
That aren't so high
That I can use to get there.
Getting old
Sucks.

I am old, you know that.
I am old, and you worry.
I am old, so you look for me.
I am old, and you call out my name.
I am old, so I sleep a lot.
I am old, so I wake you up at 4 am
I am old, and do that so you know
I am old, and want you to know I'm all right.
I am old, and you're welcome.

The Woman said:
The flipside of doubt
Is faith
And the flipside of here
Is there
So I thought:
That the flipside of no
Is yes
And the flipside of hate
Is love
And the flipside of death
Is life
Then I grasped:
That the flipside of the horizon
Is a circle
And neither ever end.

All the flipsides:
Bad to good
Empty to full
Nothing to everything
And everything?
No matter what
Everything is always,
One way or the other
Totally awesome
Because the flipside
Will take you there
Even when it's over
Because it really just began.

There was this guy on TV
Who said he was a man of faith
He wore a funky collar
But not like mine, or even a dog's
And he said that pets
The four legged furballs
That make a person's life have meaning
Don't go to heaven
Because they don't have souls
And I sat there and listened to him
Wondering from where he was getting
All of his information
Because he got the facts all wrong
Or perhaps he just didn't understand
That heaven is not heaven without everyone
And the bits and pieces of bone and fur
And the skin and the lips and the tongue and the heart
Are just the container and not the self
I do not have a soul
I *am* the soul.

The other cat that lives here
Never got to meet the dog.
The dog left for the Bridge
A year before the cat was born.

I don't much care for dogs;
They're loud and big and hairy,
But I liked my dog.
He was quiet and big and hairy.

The people loved him
Even though they thought he was dim.
"Not quite bright," they said,
"But as sweet as sweet ever gets."

I don't think they were paying attention.
As dogs go, he was spectacular.
He just understood something,
A thing people do not get.

He knew that life was finite
When his happiness was not.
He knew that joy is not just for puppies
Or even kittens, as it were.

Goofy fun is always best
And that was wrapped around his heart.
So he goofed around stupidly
And never cared what anyone thought.

But even when he was goofy
He was always kind to me
He never sat on me
Or tried to ride me like a horse.

The other cat that lives here
Would be a better man if he had only
Had the chance to know the dog
Even for a little while.

I do not want another dog
I don't even want the other cat
But he's here, so I tolerate
As best I can, and I remember

There were lessons from the dog
That I should never forget
That kindness matters
Even when the other cat annoys me.

I don't always do well
At remembering that important thing.
I growl at him a lot
And hiss and spit and swipe.

If he had only had the chance
To know the dog a while
I wouldn't have to
Because he would have learned.

When I am gone
At the Bridge, seeing the dog
And the Cat Who Came Before Me
I hope the other cat remembers

I was not the best but I did try
And I never wanted him to go away
Because he deserved a forever home
Even if it was mine.

And I hope the other cat looks back
And recalls all the times I didn't do
The things I could have done
When he was being mean.

He's a spastic cat
And truly not bright
But I hope he remembers me
The way I remember the dog.

74

I am not worried about the day
When I travel gentle in to that dark night
It might be tomorrow
But it might be a year away
Or five—who knows?
But I do not worry and I do not fear
Because I have done my job well
And in living I have given purpose
To the lives of my people
There's the Next Big Thing waiting for me
It might be a bridge, it might be something else
But it will be good
And waiting there will be all my friends
The ones who went before me
Along with the dog I really liked
And the Cat Who Came Before Me
And the Cat Who Came Before Her
Birds and squirrels and bugs
Who played outside my windows
Just to entertain me
And when I get there
To the bridge or the whatever else
I will be able to tell them Thank You
And I missed you
And I love you
And we will wait there together

For the people whom we trusted
So that they won't be as afraid
Being people, they'll need us there
As much as they need us here
So I am not worried and I am not afraid
Because I will rest
And I will relax
And I will have fun
And I will wait, because my job is not done
Not even once I have stepped
With all four of my feet
Into that gentle, sleepy good night
I will go with peace
I will get my reward
And it will be *glorious*.

You talk a lot about dying, she said
It scares me when you do
Because it makes me think there's something wrong
And that you will leave us
Sooner instead of later,
Like there's something you know
But are sparing us of the pain.

Right now I am fine
I am fat and happy and healthy
Content to stay here where I can annoy the people
And the other cat
Eating good food and treats
Watching Doctor Who
Sitting on the Woman's squishy lap.

But I admit, I talk about it
I ponder that Good Night
Turning it over in my head in order to really see it
Thinking about the dog who's there
And the Cat Who Came Before Me
Wondering about my friends

So, so many who are there.
I think about dying
But it's not a fear
And I don't worry about what comes after this
Because I'm pretty sure I know
Though I am in no hurry
There's still so much right here.

I think about dying, I talk about dying
And I am not afraid of it
But yes, I do talk about the joys that come next
Because I don't want you to be afraid
Because I don't want you to grieve
Because I am still so very much alive.

Today is the oldest I have ever been
So I will take long naps
And eat good food

Today is the youngest I will ever be again
So I will chase the red dot
And run and jump

Today is the day to do everything
Because I am old
And I am young

Because tomorrow
Will be today
All too soon.

The knife wound to your heart
Searing, blinding, burning
The pain that feels eternal:
It will be okay.

The day it becomes okay
Might not be today
Or tomorrow, or next week
But it will come.

First you will breathe
Without that jagged edge
And then you will sigh,
Exhaling a cloud of Missing You.

There will be a hole in your heart
Cat-shaped, dog-shaped,
Filled with shadows
And maybe some tears.

But then something will happen
A kitten, perhaps
Maybe a puppy
All floppy-footed and dopey.

Guilt might shoot right through you
Because it feels like betrayal
But it's not
One love does not cancel the other.

Grief is not forever
And love doesn't die
Just because you give another
A needed forever home.

It will be okay.
It will be okay.
It will be okay.
Swearsies.

Yesterday I watched someone's heart break
It was online and I was reading
But I could see it all the same.
The tiny crack that formed
Breaking open, leaving a hole
Shaped exactly like a cat.
There was talk of the Bridge
How they would meet again, all too soon
And many words of "I'm sorry."
Then I read how it was not fair
That no one should have to feel those feels
And I thought that while I understood
The pain behind those words
I knew it wasn't quite true.
I also remembered reading many times
That life itself is not fair
And sometimes it seems that way
And yet, it is.
We're born into hope and promise
And we live and breathe and love

We eat and drink and play
Knowing that someday it will all go away.
We all know that some lives are shorter,
Some lives are harder,
And that certainly does suck.
There will come a day,
Sooner rather than later,
When I will eat my dinner and then go to sleep
And I will awaken somewhere else.
Or I will vomit on a shoe and not stop
Or I will grow a lump or feel a flutter in my chest
And then in a day or week or month
I will close my eyes one last time
Exhale
And I will be gone.
My people will cry and miss me
And the pain will be real
Like a hot knife stuck into their hearts
Just so
And it will suck.

But I got to be here,
Even for a day
And I got to feel what being alive is like
I got to draw in air
And feel all of the feels.
The clock ticked on
One minute, one day, one year
Breathing in, breathing out
By luck I drew the long straw
And it's been a very long life
But it very well could have been short
Yet even so
When it was messy
And wonderful
Heartbreaking
Glorious
It was fair.
It was always fair.

(Admit it, you were waiting for this one...)

There once was a cat from Nantucket
Who kept his toys in a blue bucket
From online he done thieved it
From a walrus who grieved it
But he liked it, so said, oh well —

This page was going to say
This page intentionally left blank
But then by saying that
The page is no longer blank
But people need to know
When a blank page is meant to be blank
So that they don't think something is missing
But what's missing is a way
To say
THERE'S NOT SUPPOSED TO BE ANYTHING HERE
Without putting something there
So here you go
A blank page left unblank
Just so that I could tell you:

Yo

The book is over
I wrote the poems
I hope they were mostly okay
Now go outside and get some fresh air
Because you're kind of pale
Or watch Doctor Who
Because he is awesome
Or go play with the kitties
Or puppies
Or sticky people
But go do something fun

Because life is short

And the page isn't blank

But you can write on it if you want.

This page isn't really blank, either.

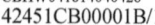
Lightning Source LLC
Chambersburg PA
CBHW041814040426
42451CB00001B/1